RUTH BADER GINSBURG

Table of Contents

Introduction

Ruth Bader Ginsburg is one of the best-known justices of the Supreme Court of the United States. Her appointment to the bench was possible because of her national reputation as an attorney. Long before becoming the second woman appointed to the highest court in America, she had spent decades fighting against gender discrimination and fighting for gender equality under the law.

Ginsburg was raised in a loving, supportive family. However, she is no stranger to personal tragedy and difficult challenges. She lost her mother to cancer the day before her high school graduation. And when her husband was diagnosed with cancer, she had to maintain a balance between the rigors of law school and the responsibilities of child-rearing by giving up sleep.

When her stellar grades earned her a seat at Harvard Law School, she was one of just nine women in a graduating class of 500 students. One day, the dean of the school asked why she was there - taking the place of a man. The rest of her life has been an emphatic answer to that question.

Ginsburg gained increasing recognition for her legal accomplishments, eventually being appointed by President Jimmy Carter to the United States Court of Appeals for the District of Columbia Circuit in 1980. Thirteen years later, she was appointed by President Bill Clinton to the United States Supreme Court in 1993. As a member of the Supreme Court, she has gained national recognition. She never missed a day of oral arguments from the day she took the bench in 1993 until 2018 when she began treatment for cancer. Since joining the court, she has regularly been among the most prolific questioners of the attorneys arguing before the court.

Despite frequent predictions that she will be the next justice to leave the Court, she has shown no real signs of slowing down. Though she has been considered a controversial figure by some, it is difficult to deny her tenacity in fighting for what she thinks is right, despite some fierce opposition.

Chapter 1

Early Life

Joan Ruth Bader was born to Nathan and Celia Bader on March 15, 1933. Though she was born in the United States, her father moved from Ukraine to America when he was young and spoke no English when he arrived. Her mother was born in New York, but her parents had moved from Austria to America only four months before her birth. Ginsburg has used herself to illustrate what immigrants are hoping for when they come to America. As the daughter and granddaughter of immigrants, she is grateful for the opportunities afforded to her. Her parents instilled a work ethic and impressed upon her the importance of education and independence in her struggles to reach her full potential.

She grew up in a loving home in Brooklyn, New York, during the Great Depression. Her father, Nathan Bader, managed to stay employed as a furrier - a person who deals in furs. To ensure their family had enough money to provide for their needs, her mother, Celia Bader, had a job in a garment factory. Joan Ruth Bader was their second daughter, but they lost their first daughter to meningitis when Joan was just 14 months old. It was the first of several deaths in the young Joan's life, but she was too young to understand at the time.

With two parents working, the small family could survive without suffering the levels of poverty that many other Americans suffered at the time. However, it did mean that there was not as much time for taking care of the family since they were a working-class family. Still, Celia knew the importance of education, so she instilled a love of learning and the importance of family in her child. Celia did not attend college herself, instead opting to work to help pay for her brother's education. The future Supreme Court Justice learned at a very early age how to prioritize the needs of others and the importance of sacrifice. Her mother's willingness to ensure that her younger brother received an education to improve his prospects definitely influenced her young daughter.

Celia also did not see education as something that benefited one gender over the other. Celia had chosen not to go to college herself so that her brother could attend, but she ensured that her children grew up loving learning, giving them an advantage when the Great Depression finally ended. She encouraged all of her children to value both education and independence, lessons that her second daughter took to heart.

During her early public education, she began to go by her middle name, Ruth, in large part because there were so many Joans in the class that it made it easier to distinguish her from the other girls with the same name. The family was religious, and she was taken to the synagogue as a part of their regular schedule. It was school where she really excelled, though, earning high marks for her work. She was also involved in several different student activities.

She had established herself as an excellent student by the time she started attending James Madison High School. The future Justice stood out as an exceptional student. Unfortunately, the woman who had instilled her interest in learning did not see her daughter's graduation from high school. Celia was diagnosed with cancer around the time her daughter began high school. After fighting cancer for several years, Celia died the day before Ruth's high school graduation. Ruth did not attend her high school graduation as she was preparing for her mother's funeral. This was the first of several tragic events in the future Justice's life, a sign of the kinds of adversity and setbacks that she often overcame during her life.

Joan Ruth Bader was accepted into Cornell University with a full scholarship. She had just started college when she met Martin Ginsburg. He would later say that he was drawn to the young woman's intellectual abilities and continued pursuit of learning. In her professional life, Ruth was heavily influenced by Vladimir Nabokov, a Russian writer, by Robert Cushman, a constitutional lawyer, and by her husband. All three of these men helped shape the woman she became.

Chapter 2

Education

Early in her career as a student at Cornell University, Ruth had two professors who significantly influenced her. Vladimir Nabokov was a published author. He was articulate, and his ideas were well-considered before he put pen to paper. This helped Ruth to learn how to write her opinions when she became a judge. Another professor, Robert Cushman, played a more direct influence on her future as he was a constitutional lawyer. His passion inspired her, and it led to her decision to pursue a career in law.

Ruth married her college sweetheart and moved away from New England to Oklahoma for a couple of years while Marty served his time in the army. When they returned in 1956, she applied to Harvard Law School, where her husband was already enrolled. This was the first time she faced sexism as some men claimed that her role in life was as a wife and mother, and not as a serious legal professional. They accused her of taking the seat in law school away from a man who actually needed it to make a living. This experience fostered her future in fighting for gender equality. The young woman took her education very seriously, and she did not allow anything to distract her from learning and excelling in her work. One of the most relevant lessons she learned from her time at Harvard was that she had entered an extremely male-dominated field that was openly hostile toward women. She was one of just nine women in a graduating class of 500 people at Harvard Law School.

Despite the discrimination that she faced, Ginsburg finished all of her coursework and became one of the editorial staff for the prestigious *Harvard Law Review*. She was the first woman to hold a position on the law review. However, after two years at Harvard, she left to move to New York City with her husband, who had graduated from Harvard Law School and taken a job in New York.

She applied and was accepted to Columbia Law School. Like at Harvard, she was the first woman to serve on the Columbia Law Review. While at Columbia Law School, Bader managed to balance her rigorous academic schedule while taking care of her daughter and attending to her beloved husband, Marty, who had been diagnosed with cancer. She managed to finish at the very top of her graduating class, and, after three years of law school, she earned her law degree in 1959.

Given her impressive resume, Ginsburg should have been highly sought after by numerous law firms. However, there were no federal anti-discrimination laws in place at the time. The barriers to her finding gainful employment proved to be a much harder fight, but it was one that the young mother was more than equipped to take on. She had a good relationship with the professors at Columbia, and one of them helped her to get a position.

Chapter 3

Marriage and Children

Ruth and Marty went on a blind date during her first semester at Cornell. He was also a student at Cornell, and they got along well from the start. His son later said that one of Marty's first impressions of his future wife was that she was cute. By the end of the date, he was far more impressed by how smart she was. Unlike many men at the time, he was intrigued by her intellectual pursuits, and he always encouraged her in her pursuits. They began dating in college, getting closer over their time together, even after he graduated from Cornell and went to Harvard Law School. She has said that he was the only man she ever dated who cared about her intelligence. This was one of the reasons why she was so interested in him. It would certainly be something that would help establish a remarkably harmonious relationship as they weathered the storms of life together.

They waited until after her graduation from Cornell in 1954 before they married, although they did not wait long. Just nine days after she received her bachelor's degree, they married. His education was soon interrupted by the draft.

Soon after his first year at Harvard, Ruth's new husband was drafted into the US Army. When he was stationed in Oklahoma, Ruth joined him, spending two years in the state. During this time, they had their first child, Jane. Once his time of service ended, they moved back to New England to resume his education at Harvard. Not one to simply sit by while her husband attended school, Ruth also applied to get into Harvard Law School. With her exceptional performance at Cornell University, she got in. She managed to reach the top of the class while also being a wife and mother. Her daughter, Jane, was one when Ruth started at Harvard; she was four when Ginsburg finished getting her law degree from Columbia Law School.

This was not the only significant personal problem that Ginsburg faced while working toward her degree. Her husband was diagnosed with cancer soon after they had started their time back at Harvard. The treatment was very intensive, leaving him unable to do much while he was going through it. This was followed by rehabilitation. Ginsburg had taken her mother's lessons to heart and cared for her daughter and her husband - all while achieving the highest marks at Harvard. She also made sure to take notes in her husband's classes, and she helped him to keep from falling too far behind in his studies. After Marty's recovery, he finished his Law degree at Harvard and quickly got a law firm position in New York City. Ruth moved to New York with him. She was accepted to Columbia Law School and transferred there for her final year of law school. She managed to balance school and being a mother, even after being elected to the law review.

While fighting for the right to have a job in her professional life, Ginsburg continued to have a very successful personal life. She had a son in 1965, and they named him James. She wore baggy clothing to work to hide the fact that she was pregnant because, after finding employment, she was afraid of losing her job because of her pregnancy.

Her husband proved that he was far more progressive than many of the men of the time. He loved cooking. When her daughter pointed out that he was the better cook and wanted to eat his cooking all of the time, he accepted the challenge. He did a lot more around the house than most men do today, and it was nearly unheard of at the time. Marty and Ruth were the co-leaders of their home.

Ruth was still very engaged in her children's lives, applying some of the same requirements to their school work as she had applied to her own. Jane Ginsburg once said that "she made me rewrite every English paper multiple times. That kind of paid off the other way round, when she gave me the drafts of her briefs, and I got to read them and make editing suggestions." Jane went on to earn her degree from Harvard Law school. She is currently a professor at Columbia University, teaching literary and artistic property law. James Ginsburg followed a more artistic route, though he did attend law school. Today, he runs a classical music label. His mother is a huge fan of opera, which likely helped shape his own interest in music. He started his business in 1989 when he was in his first year at law school. While in school, he launched Cedille Records, the label he still runs today. He is married to a composer and singer. He has also created a tribute song to his mother that details her life story.

Ginsburg has a granddaughter, Jane's daughter, named Clara, who also has earned a Harvard Law degree and works as a federal law clerk. Clara remembers having her third birthday party at the Supreme Court of the United States. She says that her mother, Jane, had wanted to impress upon her from an early age that anything was possible for a woman – there were two women on the Supreme Court at the time, including Clara's grandmother.

Jane also has a son, Paul, who is an actor. He and his wife have a young son, Ruth's first great-grandchild.

Over the decades, Marty supported his wife both at home and in their professional lives. He helped to lobby for her as she moved up in the court systems. He helped to impress upon their children how men should also be responsible for the chores and child-rearing. When his wife was diagnosed with cancer twice, he stayed with her in the hospital during her treatments. He even noticed when she was having an adverse reaction during a blood transfusion, and he immediately spoke up, potentially saving her life. He provided moral support to her as well. Their relationship has received much attention because he was far more willing to be a partner than the family head. The marriage has been pointed to as being idyllic because of how unusually happy they were. Unfortunately, Marty was again diagnosed with cancer, and he died in 2010.

Chapter 4

Early Career

When Ruth Bader Ginsburg graduated from Columbia Law School in 1959, there were no federal anti-discrimination laws. So when she applied for a position with several different law firms, the men who did the hiring at the law firms were very blunt about why they were not willing to hire her. They told her they did not want any female lawyers at their firms. Ginsburg came to view her problems with getting a job as being a result of three factors about her.

1. She was Jewish. Many of the law firms were resistant to hiring Jewish lawyers.
2. She was a woman. This was frequently confirmed as a significant strike against her in terms of her employability.
3. She was a mother. This kind of discrimination was legal, common, and something that she feared when she became pregnant with her second child.

As she had found at Harvard, the legal profession was very much a male-dominated field, and many men did not want that to change. At that time, only two women had served on any of the federal circuits, and no one had ever reached the highest position of Supreme Court Judge.

Fortunately, one of her professors from Columbia, Gerald Gunther, helped her get a position working as a clerk for Judge Edmund Palmieri, a US District Court judge for southern New York. He was able to get her the position with what she described as a stick and carrot approach. The carrot was that if she did not perform to Judge Palmieri's satisfaction, the professor would have a male graduate lined up and ready to take over for her. The stick was if the judge did not give her a chance, the professor would not recommend any more Columbia Law School graduates to assist him. The judge did accept her, giving Ginsburg her first professional job after graduation. She worked as a clerk for the US District Court for the Southern District of New York from 1959 to 1961.

Her options were limited when she left the position in 1961. Looking back on that time, she has talked about how the timing of her entry into the field changed the trajectory of her career. Had she been able to get a job with one of the law firms, she would likely be a retired law firm partner now. Since law firms were unwilling to hire a woman, she ended up taking a position as the associate director of the Project on International Procedure at Columbia Law School. She held the position from 1962 until 1963. During this time, she focused on Swedish civil procedure, resulting in the publication of *Civil Procedure in Sweden*, which was co-authored by Anders Bruzelius, in 1965. This was her first book.

Ginsburg left the position in 1963 when she was offered a position as an assistant professor at Rutgers School of Law. The offer came with the request that she be willing to accept less pay than her male peers because she had a husband who had a better paying job. It was during her time working at Rutgers that she became pregnant with her son. Since she was on a contract with the school, she was afraid that they would let her contract run out and not renew it because of her condition. To hide her pregnancy, she began to wear baggier clothing. Eventually, the college showed her some support as they granted her tenure in 1969.

During her time as a tenured professor at Rutgers, Ginsburg began to fight for gender equality. She came to put a heavy emphasis on a person's record and capabilities over gender and connections.

Chapter 5

Joining the Fight for Gender Equality

After more than a decade of dealing with gender discrimination, Ginsburg finally joined in the growing fight for women's rights in 1970. Her entry into the battle was relatively small. She was asked to serve as the announcer and moderator at a law student panel. The topic of the discussion was women's liberation. Though she had faced much external discrimination, Ginsburg also had much support from her professors, who knew what she was capable of. More importantly, she had a very supportive husband who was willing to help her in any way that he could. This was something that many other women around the US did not and still do not have. Many husbands felt that their wives should only work as a hobby.

By 1971, Ginsburg had fully jumped into the fight, published articles in law reviews, and was an instructor at a seminar focused on the problems and solutions to gender discrimination. During the seminar, she began to work with the American Civil Liberties Union (ACLU). She worked with the ACLU to draft briefs that were used in two separate federal cases. Her husband brought the first case to her attention, which adversely affected men. The idea that women were the principal caregivers was so ingrained that any single man who was the caregiver in his family was denied the tax deduction that single women could access. Ginsburg fought for gender equality, regardless of which gender was being discriminated against. The other brief focused on a law in Idaho. At the time, Idaho had a law that openly gave preference to men as the person who administered the estate of someone who was deceased if that person did not leave a will. Men were allowed to manage the estate, even if there was a woman with a much better claim to being the administrator. This law made it easier for men to leave wives and daughters with far less of an inheritance than they should have gained following the death of a husband or father. This was the *Reed v. Reed* case that was ruled on by the US Supreme Court in 1971, and it was the first time that a statute that discriminated against a gender was struck down by the court.

After this introduction to legal proceedings, Ginsburg began to get more engaged in the more practical side of her field. Over the 1970s, she became one of the most notable figures fighting against gender discrimination. She continued her work with the ACLU, becoming one of the founding counsels for their Women's Rights Project. She also was the co-author of a casebook for law schools that discussed gender discrimination.

Ginsburg has said that she sometimes felt like a preschool teacher when presenting her arguments to the male establishment. To them, there was nothing wrong with the way things had always been, and that a woman's place was in the home. Ginsburg ingeniously couched the argument from a very different perspective. Where men wanted their mothers and wives to support them from the home, they wanted something more from their own children. She swayed them by pointing out that they were limiting the potential of their daughters, often changing the minds of men who wanted to see their daughters succeed. They began to see how women were limited and how much of a struggle it would be for their own daughters because so many other men viewed women the same way.

Chapter 6

Speaking Before the Highest Court

While changing the minds of the male boards and institutions, she was offered and accepted a tenured position at Columbia Law School. She was the first woman to hold a tenured position at the school. She held this position from 1972 until 1980. Over those eight years, Ginsburg was prolific in writing law review articles and helping to draft or contribute to drafts of briefs to go to the Supreme Court, most of which focused on gender discrimination. It was also her first experience with the Supreme Court as she spoke in front of the all-male justices six times. She and the legal teams won five of those cases.

Frontiero v. Richardson – The case was argued and decided in 1973. Sharron Frontiero sued to get a dependent's allowance for her husband. Because she was a member of the US Air Force, this was a federal case. The federal laws automatically granted the wives of service members an allowance, but women had to prove that their husbands depended on them for at least 50% of their support. The Supreme Court ruled that this discrimination was a violation of the Fifth Amendment's Due Process Clause. The reasoning for why this was the case was far more varied, so there was no majority opinion; there were a couple of opinions issued as a part of the review. A plurality of the court found that the gender discrimination was comparable to racial discrimination, making it illegal. The other opinion said that the gender discrimination was not comparable to racial discrimination, saying that the discrimination was too arbitrary, which was disallowed by the Constitution.

Weinberger v. Wiesenfeld – The case was argued and decided in 1974. This was a case in which a widower was denied Social Security benefits. Unlike the other case, the wife actually had been the primary source of income for the family. When she died in childbirth and her widower applied for survivor's benefits, he was denied, though his newborn son could receive benefits. Like the previous case, the Justices ruled in favor of the widower, saying that the justifications to withhold benefits to the widower were both counter-productive and illogical.

Kahn v. Shevin – The case was argued and decided in 1974. Florida's laws gave widows a $500 property tax exemption but did not apply that same exemption to widowers. Mel Kahn sued the Dade County Tax Assessor's Office to get the benefits. The Supreme Court ruled against Kahn because they found that widows were at a significant financial disadvantage following the death of their husbands. They often had to begin working, earning less in wages than their husbands. The tax exemption was meant to provide some assistance given the widow's financial hardships. Men did not face the same financial hardships, so the court ruled they did not require the same assistance.

-

Edwards v. Healy – The case was argued in 1974 and decided in 1975. The Louisiana Constitution required women to apply to serve on juries. The state made changes to its constitution, so this case was treated as moot since the problem was resolved by those changes.

Califano v. Goldfarb – The case was argued in 1976 and decided in 1977. This is another case where discrimination against men had caused harm. The widower, Leon Goldfarb, had applied for survivor's benefits after his wife passed away. She had paid into Social Security for more than 25 years before her passing, but when her husband applied for benefits under the *Social Security Act*, he was denied. At the time, men could only qualify for survivor's benefits if their wives had provided at least half of the familial support (something that was very unlikely in 1976). The same requirement was not applied to women. It was widely assumed that women were dependent on their husbands, so it was likely felt that it was not necessary at the time of writing of the *Act*. The Supreme Court agreed with the state of New York, which had deemed this requirement unconstitutional. The ruling was 5 to 4, with the majority rejecting what they called an "archaic and over-broad" generalization about a woman's dependence on her husband, saying that "old notions" of what role a person served based on genders was not adequate to justify discriminating against survivors of a deceased spouse.

Duren v. Missouri – The case was argued in 1978 and decided in 1979. The defendant, Billy Duren, said that the court system had violated both his Sixth and Fourteenth Amendment rights by having a heavily male-dominated jury. At the time, Missouri allowed women to be exempt upon request. While women comprised 54% of the district, only five women were in the jury wheel, leading to an all-male jury. The Supreme Court reversed the state's decision, saying that the statistics provided by Duren's lawyers showed that the state had violated their client's rights.

As is evident in the cases for which Ginsburg wrote, she fought as hard for equality for men in a system that placed certain expectations on them that were not present for women. At the time, it was easier to start to break down gender discrimination by upsetting expectations, and the nation was better equipped to see how it was wrong to discriminate against men simply because of their gender. From jury pools to benefits, denying men a fair trial by excluding women or denying them the benefits that their wives had earned was wrong. It was then easier to point out how the same kind of discrimination against women, but on a much larger scale, was similarly wrong. It was necessary to admit that there was a problem before trying to affect significant changes.

Chapter 7

Appointment to US Court of Appeals

Having earned a reputation after a decade of arguing for gender equality, Ginsburg caught the attention of President Jimmy Carter. He was impressed by her record, appointing her to the US Court of Appeals for the District of Columbia in 1980. Her abilities quickly gained her a reputation in the circuit as a pragmatic liberal. She was considered intelligent and open to well-thought arguments. Her ability to put aside work also gained her much respect from both sides. She served at the same time as Robert Brok and Antonin Scalia, two notoriously conservative judges. She later served on the US Supreme Court with Scalia. During this time, the three judges acknowledged their differences but could respect the position of the others. While it was not exactly a friendship, Ginsburg had a cordial relationship with the two men who more often than not disagreed with her perspectives.

The year after Ginsburg was appointed to serve on the US Court of Appeals in DC, Sandra Day O'Connor was chosen by President Ronald Reagan to be the first woman to serve on the US Supreme Court.

Ginsburg served on the circuit court until 1993. At the end of her time, she delivered a lecture to the students at the New York University Law School, where she was somewhat critical of the highly controversial decision handed down in *Roe v. Wade* in 1973. Though the ruling had initially been largely ignored, over time, she watched as it was increasingly politicized and became the controversial issue that it is today. During the lecture, she said that it would have been better if the Supreme Court had issued a more limited decision about abortion instead of something so sweeping in scope. This would have given states the ability to establish their own details about abortions. By giving states some room to control how to address abortion, she felt that it "might have served to reduce rather than to fuel controversy." This would have made it likely that more cases would have been submitted to the Supreme Court much earlier, but it would have avoided the division and discord that has been sown by the blanket ruling. Her decisions have reflected more of an incremental approach instead of forcing people to pick and cling to a side.

Chapter 8

Second Woman on the US Supreme Court

Ginsburg's reputation proceeded her. President Bill Clinton nominated her for the US Supreme Court on June 14, 1993. Clinton selected her as a way of countering the very conservative members of the Court at the time. When the nomination process began, it was reported that the Senate Judiciary Committee was particularly friendly with her, reflecting how she was able to talk to both sides. There were a few senators who expressed some frustration with the way she was able to evade directly answering some hypothetical situations. Some senators were also concerned that her work fighting as a social advocate would not be put aside if she were appointed to the highest court in the land. However, those concerns were not strong enough to deny her skills or abilities. She was quickly confirmed, with the US Senate voting 96 to 3 for her confirmation.

Ironically, Ginsburg was the nominee who argued that it was a person's record and abilities that should determine whether they were fit for the Court, and not their party or views. This was likely why she was confirmed so quickly. When considered on the merits of her abilities, it was nearly impossible to deny she was more than qualified for the position.

She became the second woman to sit on the bench. As mentioned in a previous chapter, Sandra Day O'Connor was the first woman to reach the most powerful position in the Judiciary branch in 1981. This meant that the first two women served together for more than a decade, and neither shied away from speaking up when they felt it was necessary. The first case that Sandra Day O'Connor heard was *Mississippi University for Women v. Hogan*, and she ended up writing the majority opinion. Hogan was suing the all women's school for discriminating against him because he was male. The Court ruled that the school would have to admit him because he was qualified, and it was illegal to deny him entrance because of his gender. Ginsburg's career mirrored this, with her writing the majority opinion for the *United States v. Virginia*. This case saw a woman being denied entry into the Virginia Military Institute simply because of her gender. Ginsburg wrote for the majority. Not only did Ginsburg point out that the program was unsuitable for most of the state's college students - both males and females - but she pointed out that "Generalizations about 'the way women are,' estimates of what is appropriate for *most women*, no longer justify denying opportunity to women whose talent and capacity place them outside the average description." Since the program was also too difficult for most males, meaning that it was aimed at those who were exceptional, it also targeted exceptional females; it did not disqualify women.

The two women often fell on the same side of an argument when it came to gender equality, showing that the party of the president who appointed a judge is largely irrelevant. O'Connor was appointed by a Republican, while Ginsburg was appointed by a Democrat. Once on the bench, though, politics and parties are no longer considered. Justices are meant to rule based on precedent and the Constitution. There were many things on which O'Connor and Ginsburg disagreed, but their gender gave them a very different perspective from the males on the court. Because of this, there were some issues on which they often held the same opinion.

Over the decades, Ginsburg has consistently ruled against discrimination of all kinds, though she is best known for siding against gender discrimination in particular.

She is considered a liberal justice and often concurs with more liberal decisions. However, she has repeatedly proven that opinions and rulings do not dictate how people should treat each other. Ginsburg and Scalia actually grew to become close friends, and when he died in 2016, she lost both a colleague and friend. She and O'Connor were also close, despite having some very different views on many subjects.

Ginsburg is on the record saying that she will continue to serve on the bench as long as she feels capable. When some people were upset that she did not step down while President Barack Obama was in office, she replied that justices should not base their decisions based on which party holds the presidency, an example that has not been entirely followed by other justices. She has said that the decision to leave should be based on when a justice feels the time is right for them. Currently, she is the oldest justice on the bench, though she is not the oldest in history. That distinction goes to Justice Oliver Wendell Holmes Jr., who did not retire until after his 90th birthday.

Chapter 9

The Ginsburg Precedent

Ginsburg's confirmation hearing was unique because she worked to focus on the nominee's credentials. This was based on a belief that a judge should be appointed to uphold the laws of the land, not be judged based on their views. It was this approach that frustrated some senators as they tried to figure out how she would rule on certain types of cases once she was on the bench.

There is a logic to focusing exclusively on a judge's knowledge and ability to follow the laws since the point of the judicial system is to uphold the law. Judges determine what is and is not legal based on their interpretations. While their views may help to color their decisions, the final rulings throughout history have repeatedly proven that the facts of each case significantly change the way that a person will rule. There have been many decisions that have surprised the prognosticators, and a person's credentials are a far better indicator of how they will rule rather than their own personal views.

Some people have accused Ginsburg's approach to her confirmation hearing as a way of hiding her own views. Not only were her views reasonably obvious to see from her work fighting gender discrimination over more than a decade, but she was also fairly open and honest in her answers. She avoided providing details that most job hunters are not required to give during interviews. Her answers highlighted her qualifications, methodologies as a judge in the DC circuit, and how she approached interpreting statutory and constitutional laws.

Since her confirmation, several justices have taken a similar approach to their confirmation hearings.

Some people have tried to alter the meaning of the Ginsburg precedent, putting it through a very different lens. They try to apply it to other positions, particularly appointed roles - which is vastly different as an appointee does not have to be confirmed - or to politicize it. In reality, it just refers to highlighting a person's record and not their views. Ginsburg seems to have learned how to approach a typically biased field by putting the focus on what matters instead of the surrounding arguments. She had been passed over for positions many times, despite being the better-qualified person for those positions. This likely resulted in a much more calculated and focused approach. At the time, the members of the Senate seemed to respect and agree with this approach, as have other judges who have used it for their confirmations.

Chapter 10

Notable Cases

As a member of the Supreme Court since 1993, Ginsburg has been on the bench for many notable cases. She has become famous for her well-written and often strongly worded dissenting opinions. She had read some of those opinions while on the bench to highlight how strongly she disagrees with some of the decisions made by the Court.

There are three decisions where she wrote fiery dissenting opinions. Two were issued in 2007 and pertained to women's rights. *Bonzales v. Carhart* upheld a partial-birth abortion ban, which she characterized as "alarming" because it "cannot be understood as anything other than an effort to chip away at a right [the right of women to choose to have an abortion] declared again and again by this Court." This harkens back to the opinion she expressed in 1993 when she said that it would have been far better to have taken an incremental approach. When change happens too quickly, it is much easier to chip away at it than by giving people time to really consider their ideas and let states have more of a say.

The second gendered question that came in front of the Supreme Court was actually very similar to some of the cases that she had successfully argued in the 1970s but were for women instead of men. *Ledbetter v. Goodyear Tire* ruled against Ledbetter, who sued Goodyear Tire for paying her less because she was not a man. She was suing to have her case reviewed because she had not been aware that she had the right to sue until after the short filing period had ended. In Ginsburg's dissenting opinion, she said that the reasons given for ruling against Ledbetter were against the will of Congress. Two years later, Congress appeared to agree with her with the passage of the *Lilly Ledbetter Fair Pay Act of 2009*. This was the first bill that President Barack Obama signed.

However, the best known dissenting opinion is *Citizens United v. Federal Election Commission* in 2010. The dissenting opinion was actually written by Justice John Paul Stevens (he retired from the Court later that year). He and the other three dissenting voices said that the ruling was against precedent, and it threatened "to undermine the integrity of elected institutions across the Nation." Since the ruling, Ginsburg has called it the worst decision the Court has ever made and has said that if she could overturn it, she would. The decision has been blamed for the introduction of unfettered money into the nation's election process. There has also been a growing movement to pass a Constitutional Amendment to overturn the ruling because it is viewed as giving corporations the same rights as citizens. This is seen as giving the people behind the corporations a second voice, giving them more power, as well as giving them the ability to buy politicians out in the open. It has often been cited as encouraging open corruption.

Perhaps the most pivotal ruling from her time on the bench was *Bush v. Gore* in 2000, a ruling that awarded George H.W. Bush the presidency. The state that determined the outcome of the Electoral College vote was Florida, where his brother was the governor at the time, and where issues with voting had cast doubts over which one of the two candidates had won. Initially, Bush had won by 1,784 votes, which triggered a recount. The recount reduced his count so that he only had 327 votes more than Gore. The state then began a manual recount of all of the ballots. In December 2000, the decision came in front of the Supreme Court, which was asked to review the laws that Florida had applied to the recounts. Ultimately, they ruled that Florida's Supreme Court had made a rule that was more like a law than a ruling, something that only the Florida legislature could do. The ruling was 5 to 4, with Ginsburg being one of the dissenting voices, saying that the ruling threatened the democracy because it denied every vote the same weight. They said that a recount was not the same as voting a second time and that the point of the recount was to ensure that every vote was counted. By denying a recount, some of the votes would not be counted. Typically, Ginsburg uses the phrase, "I respectfully dissent," but in this case, she simply said, "I dissent."

One of the most notable Supreme Court decisions in which Ginsburg agreed was *Obergefell v Hodges* in 2015. This case was brought to the Supreme Court by 14 couples and two men whose partners had died. They lived in four different states, making it another significant ruling that had rippling effects across the country. According to the same-sex couples and the two now single men, the states that were denying them the ability to marry were violating their 14th Amendment right to equal protection under the law. The Supreme Court ruled for the couples in a 5 to 4 vote, with the conservative Justice Anthony Kennedy siding with the liberal side. He also wrote the majority opinion, saying that "a liberty that includes certain specific rights that allow persons, within a lawful realm, to define and express their identity." The end result was that the Supreme Court legalized same-sex marriages, a right that had already been legalized in a number of states. It had caused problems across the nation as same-sex couples were not granted the same rights between different states - which had implications for their taxes, legal standing, and finances. Unlike the abortion ruling, the states had been making incremental steps toward legalization for a while by the time it reached the Supreme Court.

Chapter 11

Health and Fitness

People have been predicting for years that Ginsburg would retire from the Court, in large part because of her age and health. In addition to losing her mother and her husband to cancer, the Supreme Court Justice has been fighting cancer for about 20 years now, with her first diagnosis of colon cancer being announced in 1999. She was successfully treated at the time. Her next cancer diagnosis was in 2009. This time it was pancreatic cancer, a much more aggressive form of cancer. With her husband at her side, she was able to successfully see it go into remission for a second time.

Until 2018, she never missed a day on the bench. Ginsburg scheduled her treatments to be done before weekends and at other times when the court was out of session. That way, she never missed a day. Even after her husband died in 2010, she went into work because she said that he would want her to keep going. It was not until 2018 when she finally missed a day because of a lung cancer diagnosis. She announced in July of 2020 that she had undergone further cancer treatment.

While cancer is easily the most significant health concern for Ginsburg, people are also concerned about her age. She largely dismisses this one as an example of ageism. When people have expressed their concern about her ability to continue sitting on the Supreme Court because of cancer, she said that treatment was affecting her stamina, but her mental acuity was not affected. She has also had a heart stent put in and broken several ribs after a fall.

This has resulted in much interest in what she is doing to stay healthy. She stays more active than many other people in their 80s. Following her 2018 cancer fight, she appeared on *The Late Show* with Stephen Colbert and took him through her daily workout. This is the routine that she has attributed to her largely healthy life. By the time he had finished going through the workout and said that he was cramping by the time they finished, she seemed almost complexly unaffected by the same workout. Others have tried the same workout and found that it is far more difficult than most Americans can complete if they have not been exercising regularly before starting the regimen. This suggests that her workout is not for beginners. When asked who the most important person in her life is, she answered, "My personal trainer."

Chapter 12

A Pop Culture Icon

Ginsburg has become increasingly outspoken over time. This has helped attract a great deal of attention toward the octogenarian and gained her a huge following. People see her as a feminist hero and a popular culture icon. She is often referred to by her initials, RBG, and, more recently, has been given the nickname The Notorious RBG, based on the name used by the rapper, Notorious BIG. To her supporters, she is a legend.

She has kept her fierce independence despite pressure from the Democratic Party - who view her as one of their own – a view that she does not appear to totally agree with. She has been hailed for her refusal to step down so that another Democrat can be appointed. This shows just how strongly she believes in the separation between the Judicial and Executive Branches of government and the independence of the Justices from parties. It is this fierce independence that has gained her further admiration in today's incredibly toxic political environment.

She does not often speak in public, which has created a bit of a mystique around her until more recently. Her apparent unhappiness with the current system has gained her popularity, starting in around 2015. Her firm, well-written dissenting opinions have further gained her popularity as she often is on the same side as the majority of Americans. She is seen as saying what people feel about those rulings, particularly the things she has since said about *Citizens United*.

She has repeatedly appeared in memes that show her as a monarch fighting for the people, as a feminist fighting gender discrimination, and as a force to be reckoned with. Her apparent disinterest in recognition for doing her job has further fueled her popularity with women and younger generations. Her "Notorious RBG" nickname is very tongue in cheek while being sincere because of how unhappy Americans have been with the present system for several decades. They are looking for someone consistent to represent them, and it has made her hugely popular in the media.

Saturday Night Live often has one of their members play her, ribbing her for her height while making it clear that they hold her in rather high respect. She has become a popular Halloween costume and figure for T-shirts. Millennials tend to respect her for her positions, while women idolize her for her decades of fighting against gender inequality - even if they do not know the full extent of the discrimination that she herself faced.

She has her detractors as well, with Ginsburg's criticism of presidential candidate Donald Trump gaining her as much backlash as praise. When asked about him in an interview, she said that "He is a faker," and when asked directly about his potential election to office, she said, "I can't imagine what this place would be – I can't imagine what the country would be – with Donald Trump as our President." Many of her detractors have pointed to this as grounds for recusing herself from any decisions about him or his administration. Ginsburg herself has since said she regrets her words as she does not feel that politics are something that Justices should publicly discuss. Yet even this sentiment has gained her more appearances with the public on both sides.

The movie *On the Basis of Sex* was a biographical drama based on her life and relationship with her husband. The director admitted that he had difficulty finding financial backing for the film because so many people could not believe that a man would be as supportive as her husband was, which they claimed would make people less willing to believe or enjoy the movie.

There are two books about her life. *My Own Words* is an autobiography that became a Bestseller in 2016. In the book, she details her experiences growing up as a Jewish woman trying to work in a male-dominated field that wanted to continue to exclude women; her experiences as a working mother, and her own interpretations of the US Constitution. Like her dissents, the book is well-written as she makes her views clear. Even if the reader does not agree with those views, one can see how Ginsburg has come to hold them. There are also many quotes from people who were interviewed about her. The second book is *I Dissent* by Debbie Levy. It is a children's book aimed at letting young girls see how one woman has successfully overcome the limitations around her to become one of the most recognizable people in the US. It lets girls see that it is acceptable to disagree and think for themselves. It shows both boys and girls that there is a right way to disagree because disagreeing with others is inevitable. What is important is to do so in a respectful way. It shows Ginsburg's life through how she disagreed with different wrongs she saw throughout her long life.

Conclusion

Ruth Bader Ginsburg can be a polarizing figure. Over her long career, she has always focused on ensuring equality for everyone. Even conservatives who worked with her on the court have developed close friendships with her. People who disagree with her beliefs still respect her strong work ethic and dedication to the job. She has dealt with loss and discrimination throughout her life, but it has not defined her. Ginsburg may seem predictable, but many aspects of her life have proven to be entirely unpredictable. She is consistent in how she rules from the bench, but she does not follow traditions set by others. This shows how thoroughly she has incorporated her mother's teachings to be independent in a world that, at the time, made that incredibly difficult for women.

People will likely keep trying to predict when she will retire, a retirement that is by no means inevitable. It is possible that she will be like one of her good friends, Justice Antony Scalia, who served until his death in 2016. As some have pointed out, despite her age and health, she can still lift more than Justice Kagan and Justice Breyer. Her dedication to her health and career makes her future nearly as unpredictable as it was more than 60 years ago when she first decided to pursue a career in law.

Printed in Great Britain
by Amazon